The Ridiculousl...

Keynote for Mac

CREATING PRESENTATIONS ON YOUR MAC

Scott La Counte

ANAHEIM, CALIFORNIA
www.RidiculouslySimpleBooks.com

Copyright © 2020 by Scott La Counte.

All rights reserved. No part of this publication may be reproduced, distributed or transmitted in any form or by any means, including photocopying, recording, or other electronic or mechanical methods, without the prior written permission of the publisher, except in the case of brief quotations embodied in critical reviews and certain other noncommercial uses permitted by copyright law.

Limited Liability / Disclaimer of Warranty. While best efforts have been used in preparing this book, the author and publishers make no representations or warranties of any kind and assume no liabilities of any kind with respect to accuracy or completeness of the content and specifically the author nor publisher shall be held liable or responsible to any person or entity with respect to any loss or incidental r consequential damages caused or alleged to have been caused, directly, or indirectly without limitations, by the information or programs contained herein. Furthermore, readers should be aware that the Internet sites listed in this work may have changed or disappeared. This work is sold with the understanding that the advice inside may not be suitable in every situation.

Trademarks. Where trademarks are used in this book this infers no endorsement or any affiliation with this book. Any trademarks (including, but not limiting to, screenshots) used in this book are solely used for editorial and educational purposes.

Table of Contents

Introduction 7

The Basics 1
   How To Get Keynote 1
   Running Keynote for the First Time 3
   The Keynote Crash Course 4
      Select All Slides 7
      Select Options 8
      Cut, Copy and Paste 8
      Find and Replace 8
      Define 10
      Copy Style 11
      Inserting Hyperlinks 11
      Undo/Redo 12
   Menus 13
      Slide Menus 14
      Elements Menu 21
   Top Menus 26
      Slide Menu 26
      Play Menu 28
      View Menu 29
   Opening Keynote From iCloud 31
   Managing Documents 32
      Renaming Documents 33

Photos for Keynote 35
   Inserting An Image 36
   Arranging Images 37
      Resize and Rotate 38
      Placement 39

Image Grouping 40
Watermarks 41

Edit Mask and Alpha 42

Styling Your Image 45
Basic Styles 46
Border 46
Shadow 48
Reflection 50
Transparency 50

Tables 52

Inserting a Table 52
Adding Columns and Rows 53

Interacting with Tables 54

Row / Column Options 55

Styling Tables 55
Table Options 55
Cell Options 56
Text Options 59
Arrange Options 61

Deleting Tables 61

Importing Tables 62

Charts 63

Inserting a Chart 63

Editing Chart Data 66

Styling Your Pie Chart 67

Styling Your Bar Chart 73

Shapes 75

Inserting a Shape 76

Resizing Shapes and Adjusting Proportions 77
Moving and Rotating Shapes 78
Adding Text to a Shape 78

Creating Text Boxes 79

Styling Shapes and Text Boxes 81

Templates *82*

Using Third-Party Keynote Templates...................... 83

Creating Your Own "Templates" 83

Sharing and Exporting Document *85*

Syncing Documents with iCloud 86

Emailing a Document From Keynote 86

Collaborating 86

Export a Keynote Document 87

Exporting a Movie 88

Printing 89

The Winning Keynote Pitch Deck............................ *92*

Introduction 94
PowerPoint or Keynote 97
Getting Started: The Four Key Points to Remember 98
The Winning Pitch 100
Conclusion 116

Appendix: Keyboard Shortcuts *117*

General Keyboard Shortcuts 117

Formatting Keyboard Shortcuts 119

About the Author *122*

Disclaimer: *Please note, while every effort has been made to ensure accuracy, this book is not endorsed by Apple, Inc. and should be considered unofficial.*

INTRODUCTION

Microsoft PowerPoint *used* to rule them all. It didn't matter what computer or operating system you had—if you needed to present something, you used PowerPoint.

Times have changed! Today there are many presentation solutions out there. Some, like Google Slides, are pretty barebones; and others, like PowerPoint, feel at times feature creep—there are just so many options, it's easy to get lost. If you use a Mac, iPad, or iPhone, then you have a third option that is growing in popularity: Keynote.

In addition to being simple yet visually stunning, Keynote comes free with Apple devices. What's even better is it's pretty easy to get started even with limited knowledge of the software.

If you really want to get the most out of it, then this guide will help. It will show you the ropes—including how to do all those things you are used to doing in Microsoft PowerPoint, and help you with some of the features you may not even know about.

Ready to get started? Let's go!

[1]
THE BASICS

This chapter will cover:
- How to get Keynote
- Opening your first document
- Keynote crash course
- Formatting
- Layouts and styles

HOW TO GET KEYNOTE

Depending on how you acquired your Mac, you may or may not have Keynote already. Getting it is easy. And even better: getting it is free! (You can see if you have it by going into the Launchpad from the dock and searching for Keynote).

There's one catch: not all Macs are supported. But most are. MacOS 10.14 is required to run Keynote, which means you must have one of the following computers:
- MacBook: Early 2015 or newer
- MacBook Air: Mid 2012 or newer
- MacBook Pro: Mid 2012 or newer
- Mac Mini: Late 2012 or newer
- iMac: Late 2012 or newer
- iMac Pro
- Mac Pro: Late 2013 or newer; Mid 2010 or Mid 2012 models require a Metal-capable GPU

As long as you have one of those, then you can go to the App Store (it's in your Launchpad). Keynote is a digital download only—you cannot obtain a physical copy of it. The download is a few hundred MB.

From there, type in Keynote in the search bar, and hit the return key.

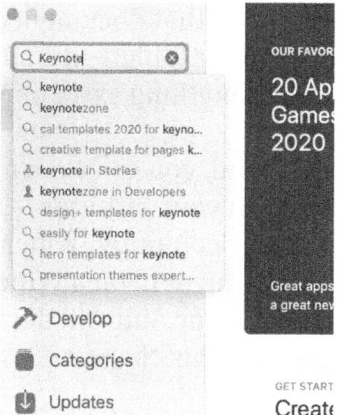

If you have it, the return result will have an Open button; if you don't have it, the result will show a Get button. When you click Get, you'll be prompted to put in your Apple ID and password; if you don't have an Apple ID, then follow the onscreen instructions to get one (it is free).

RUNNING KEYNOTE FOR THE FIRST TIME

When you first open Keynote, you'll be asked if you want to use iCloud. I recommend you do; this makes it easy to save and open documents across all devices—if you are creating a presentation on your phone, for instance, you can open that document and continue working on it from your tablet—it's all very seamless and doesn't require anything extra on your part once it's set up.

If you set up iCloud, you can even access and type in documents right in your browser— there is nothing else to install on your computer, which means "technically" you could use Keynote on a Windows computer or even a Chromebook or Android device—I'll show you how at the end of this chapter.

The Keynote Crash Course

The first time you use Keynote, you'll get a brief tutorial. You can either watch it or skip it.

Each time you open Keynote, you'll be greeted with a directory box that asks you if you want to open a document or if you want to create a new one. We'll be working off a new document in this chapter, so click "New Document" in the lower left corner.

The next box you'll see is all the available templates you can use. A template is a premade document that you can add text into. These have different styles and color choices already assigned.

The most barebones styles (meaning you'll be doing most customization of the color / style choices) are Black or White.

Before making your selection, it's important to consider how you will be presenting a presentation. Will you be presenting on a HDTV, for example? Or a projector? The reason this is important is because Keynote has two different dimensions: Standard and Wide. You can see those two dimensions at the top of the template menu.

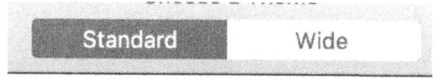

The styling of the template will stay the same, but the size ratio will be slightly different. Standard is the most universal format and ideal if you don't know how you will be presenting. Wide is best for widescreen TVs—using standard will leave black bars on the sides of the screen. Both will work, but it will fit better if you pick the right ratio prior to presenting.

First time users of Keynote are often a little disappointed the first time they use Keynote; if you've used PowerPoint, then you have ribbons and menus and options everywhere! Keynote looks pretty bare next to that.

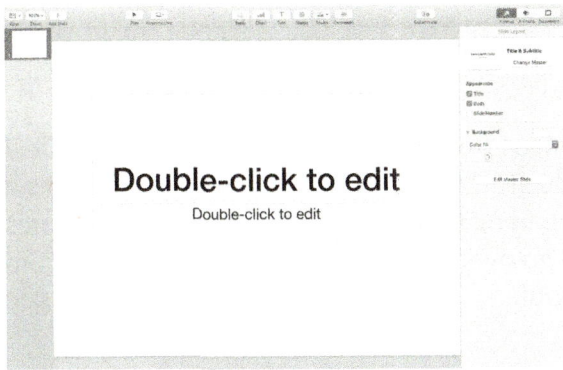

Don't worry—looks can be deceiving; there are plenty of options when you know how to find them, and I'll show you each of them in this book.

If you feel overwhelmed already because there are options, you can hide that side panel by clicking on the Format button in the upper right corner. Hint: clicking once on any of these buttons shows it, and clicking on the button again hides it.

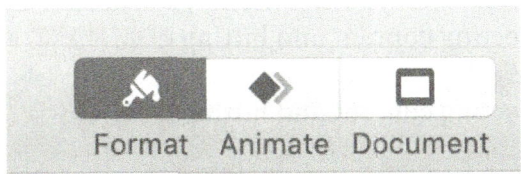

Now that you have a blank screen, let's go over the very basics of Keynote.

SELECT ALL SLIDES

Select All selects everything in your document. It's a very powerful command! It brings up the same options as Select, but any changes you make will be applied to the entire document.

To Select All, use Command + A on your keyboard.

Select Options

Once you have some content on your slide, how do you do stuff to it? If you click with two fingers on your trackpad or mouse, then the options box comes up. We'll go over what these options are as we continue in the book.

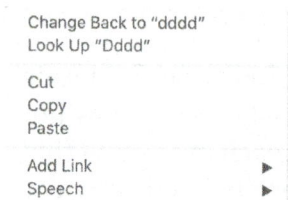

Cut, Copy and Paste

To copy and paste words (and images, tables and charts) quicker, you can use keyboard shortcuts.

Selecting content and hitting COMMAND + C will copy it.

Selecting content and hitting COMMAND + X will cut it.

And hitting COMMAND + V will copy the content anywhere you want it in the document.

Find and Replace

Find and Replace is a handy little feature in Keynote that allows you to replace your selection with alternatives.

Let's say you just created 50 slides for your big presentation on why men are mean. But once you are done, you realize the topic is not men being mean, but pigs being mean! You can change 'men' to 'pigs' in seconds!

Go to edit from your menu bar, and select Find > Find.

From here you can find all the uses of the word you want to find, but you can also click the down arrow on the left side and select Find & Replace. This lets you search for a word (top line) and replace the word once it finds it (bottom line); when you have both the find and replace word added, then you can click Replace & Find.

Define

Keynote has a handy little dictionary built in. You can select any word, tap the trackpad twice to bring up the options menu, and tap Look Up to see the definition of any word.

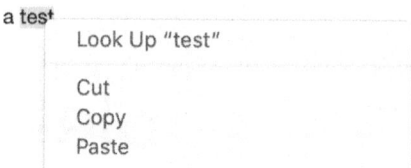

The dictionary will give you multiple definitions (and a thesaurus); even more, you can select options on the bottom to see movies related to the word, Siri Knowledge (which is encyclopedic information), apps related to it, and more!

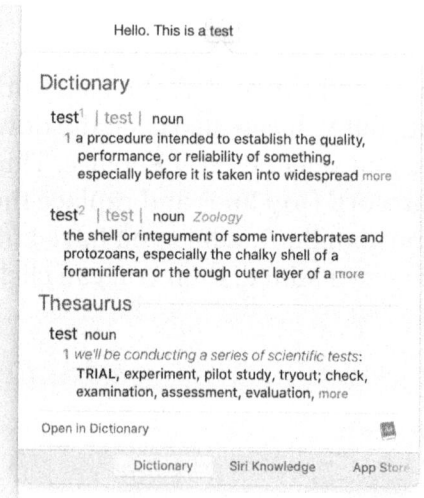

COPY STYLE

The Copy Style command lets you copy and paste styles, like the Microsoft Word format painter feature. If you ever want to make a piece of text look like another, just select the text with the format you'd like to copy, click Format > Copy Style; then select the text you want to alter and click Format > Paste Style. This can be a major time saver!

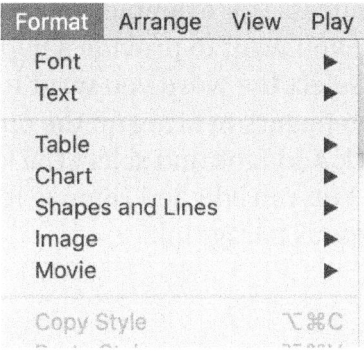

INSERTING HYPERLINKS

If you want to insert a hyperlink to an internet resource, just type out the link. Keynote automatically detects hyperlinks and will insert the link for you. To edit the link or to change the displayed text, just click the link and then tap Link Settings. Here you can edit the link itself, change the text displayed, or remove the link altogether.

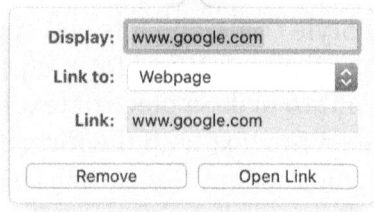

If you aren't typing a web address, but want to link it to a web address (for example, you are typing: "I go to UCLA" and you want to provide a hyperlink to UCLA), then select the word you want to hyperlink and click with two fingers to bring up the options. From here, just click Add Link and select the kind of link you want to add. You can edit and remove it the same way as in the previous paragraph.

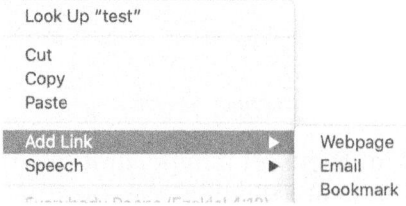

Undo/Redo

If you mess up (for example you delete a paragraph that you shouldn't have deleted) you can Undo it by going to Edit > Undo; you can also redo it under the same menu.

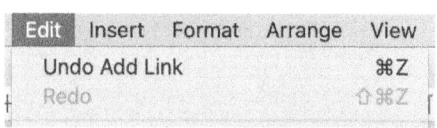

Menus

The best way to think about Keynote is in layers. This is especially true when you are working with menus.

The first layer is the slide itself; the next layers will be the elements in that slide (i.e. text boxes, graphics, bullet points, etc.).

When you take a look at the right side of your screen, you'll see three menu option icons: Format, Animate, and Document.

When I click format, I'll see a menu that looks like the graphic below.

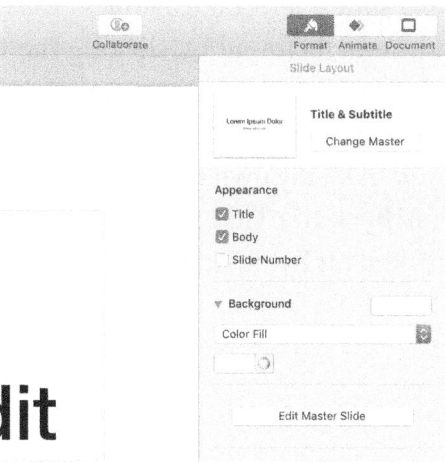

It has nothing about style or fonts, as you might expect in a format menu; that's because I haven't clicked anything. It's assuming I want to format the slide itself and not the text.

If I click the textbox inside this slide, however, the formatting menu will immediately change to something that lets me adjust the style.

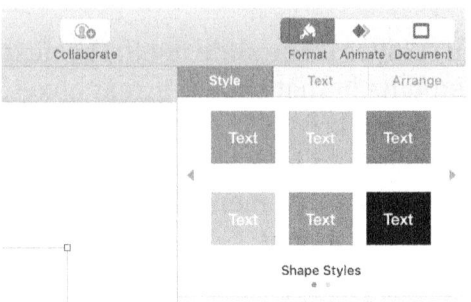

Slide Menus

Now that you understand the difference between formatting slides and formatting elements or layers within those slides, let's take a look at the Slide Menus.

The first menu is found by clicking the Format icon; this menu lets you adjust the layout of the slide. Personally, I usually prefer to work with a completely blank slide and add in all my own elements; if that sounds like you then uncheck the Title and Body boxes (which are always checked off by default).

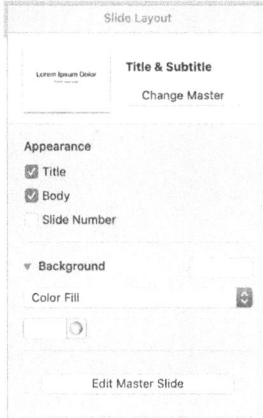

At the top of the menu is an option that says Change Master. What's that about? By default, you'll start with a title slide—in other words, a slide that lets you put the name and subtitle of your presentation. When you click Change Master, then you'll see all the possible types of slides. So, for example, you want to have a bulleted slide or a slide with a photo and bullets.

16 | *The Ridiculously Simple Guide to Keynote For Mac*

This is a more advanced topic that I won't cover in depth in this book because most people will not use it, but you can make changes to the Master Slides. At the bottom of the menu, there's a button that says Edit Master Slides. This brings up all your slide masters. You can click on any of those and add elements. Once you add them, then hit done near the bottom right corner of the screen to return to the main menu. Once the element is added, any time you change a slide to that master slide, the element will be there. It can be a major time saver if you find you are using the same type of slide over and over again.

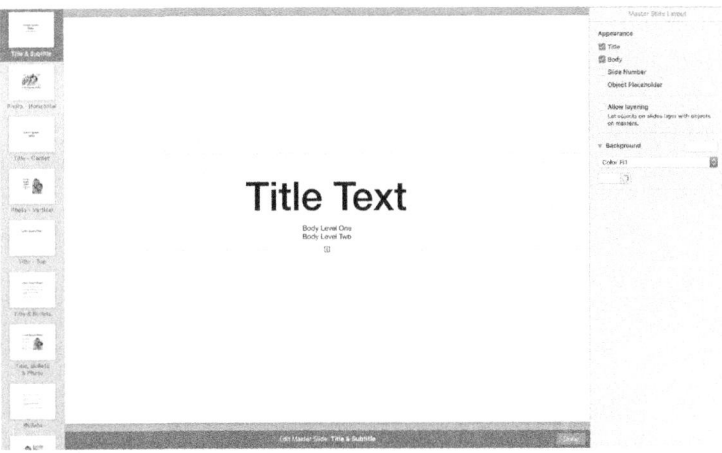

Also in the Format menu is the option to change the background; if, for example, you want to use a different color (or you want an image as the background), then you can add it in here.

The next menu is Animate. Animate is a transition to the slide; so, for example, the slide will give the appearance of falling onto the screen when it appears (or leaves). You choose for this to happen "On Click", which means it happens as soon as you click your mouse, or you can add a timed delay—which means it happens on a timer after a set amount of seconds / minutes. For most people, on click will be the way to go; using the timed feature would be ideal if you were turning your slide into a short movie (which I'll cover later).

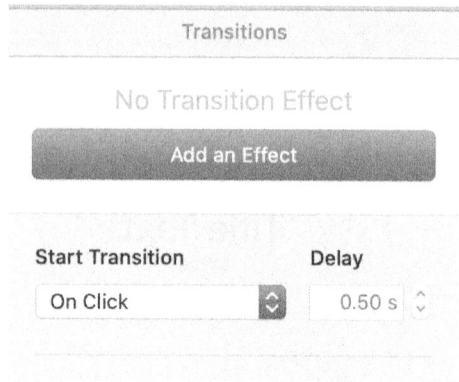

There are dozens of different animation to try. You can preview them by hovering your mouse over the name and then selecting preview.

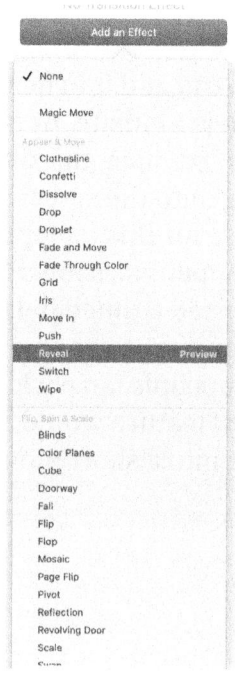

Once you make your selection, a new menu will appear with options for that animation. The options will change depending on the type of animation that's been chosen. Most will only give the option to change the direction of the animation and how the animation is started (i.e. On Click). You can also change and preview the transition at the top.

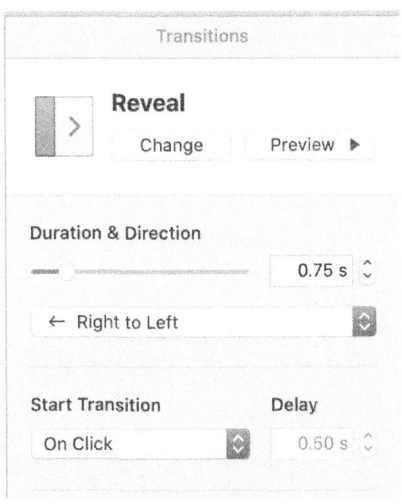

The last menu option for the slide is Document. There are two important things to note here: you can change the theme (if you chose the wrong one when you started), and, at the bottom, you can pick a different size. For example, let's say you did the presentation in 4:3, but on the day of the presentation, you found out it is going to be on a widescreen display. 4:3 will still work, but there will be black bars on the sides. So you can change the size here to fit better. Keep in mind, however, if you change the size, then it might make adjustments to the slide—moving text boxes and images over. It's always a good idea to go through your presentation one more time when changing the size.

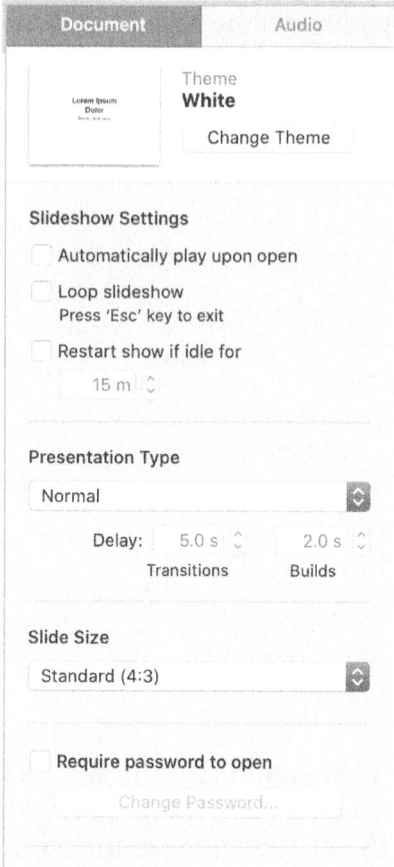

There's a second menu tab for audio in the Document menu. Most people won't use this feature. This is an excellent tool, however, if you are creating a movie from your slide so someone on the web can watch it later.

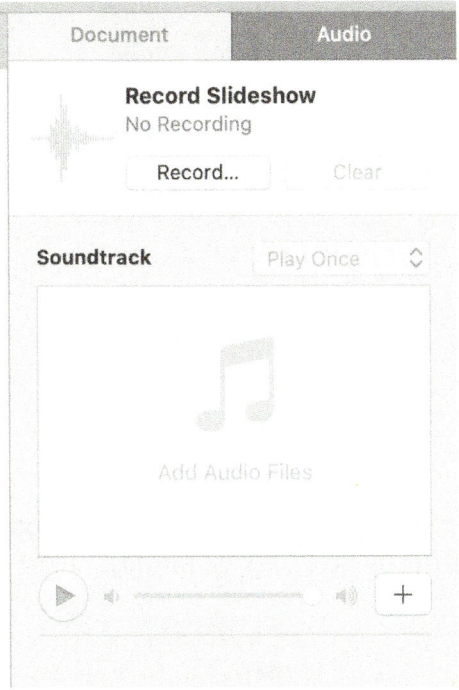

Elements Menu

The elements menus aren't very different from the slide menus; in fact, many of them are the same.

The biggest difference between them will be when you click the Format menu.

There are three tabs when you edit an element: Style, Text, Arrange (some elements, such as Images, will look slightly different and not have the Text tab).

Under style, you can add a border, fill, and add shadow to the element; what I find most useful is the Opacity option. This option adds transparency to the element, which can be useful if you are using an image behind text.

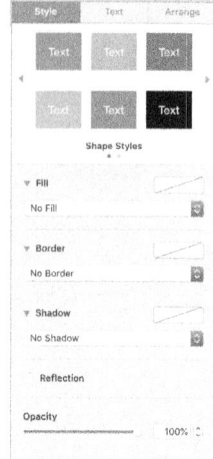

Under Text, you can change the type of text it is (a subtitle, title, or body, for example).

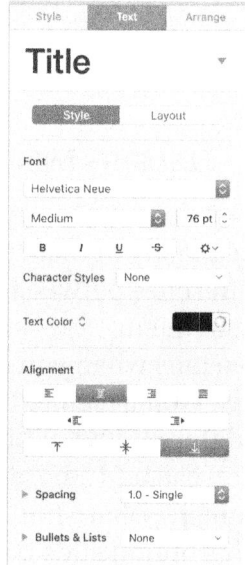

When you click it, you'll see several options. "Body" is normal text in a document—the text you are reading right here would be considered Body Text; but documents have several types of paragraph text. For example, each section of this chapter has a "Heading"—you could just change the font size and make it "look" like a heading, but using a Paragraph Style tells Keynote what kind of text it is so it can put together a table of contents later.

Some of the styles will not be very common, "Label Dark" for example.

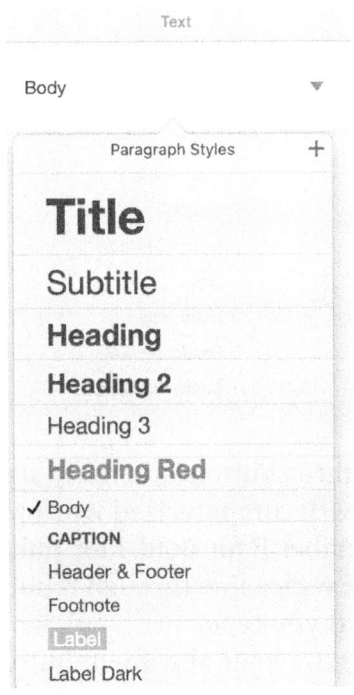

Under this are options for Style, Layout, and More. Let's stay on Style for now, so the next option is Font.

It says 11pt Helvetica; this is the font. If you tap on it, you'll be able to select a new font and adjust the size. Keynote offers a healthy font selection, including perennial favorites like Arial, Times New Roman, and Helvetica. Some notable absences include Comic Sans (and yet Papyrus still made the cut), Calibri, and Cambria.

The "regular" drop down shows you all the style choices for that font (some fonts have different options).

The next three buttons are fairly standard. If you're not familiar with computerized word processing, though, remember B for Bold, I for Italic, and U for underline. The S with a line through it puts a strike across any text you type.

Below this are your alignment buttons. Tap them for options to align your text left, center or right, or justify it. Justified text is text that fills one line exactly. Try it out to see how it works.

The next two buttons are indent buttons. Use them to indent, or to move backwards through indents.

Finally, below this is where you can add bulleted lists and line spacing (if you want to double space, for example).

The final tab is Arrange.

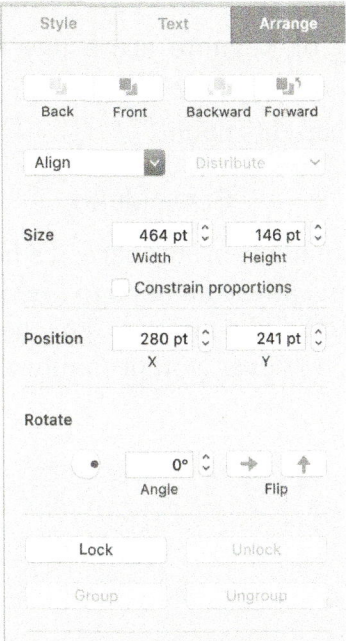

I first said to think of Keynote in terms of layers; I could have just as easily said Elements (and I have in this section); an element is a layer. The reason I use the word "layer" is because layer helps illustrate what an element can do—they can move in front and behind different elements. That's what the Arrange menu is all about. For example, let's say you want to put an image behind a text box. You can add an image to your slide and move it in front of the text box, then go here, and click the "Back" icon to send it behind the Text Box. You can also lock it in place so it can't be moved accidently.

Top Menus

At the top of Keynote are a few menus that you should understand; other menus will come up as you continue to read this book.

Slide Menu

The slide menu is pretty bare; it's helpful if you have dozens of slides and need to find it quickly, or if you want to add slide numbers. For the average presentation, however, you probably won't refer to it very often.

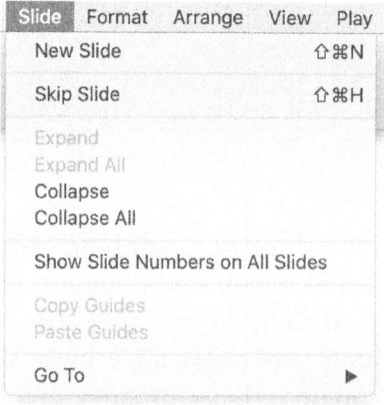

There is something worth talking more about in this menu, however: collapse. What exactly are you going to collapse? This is an organizational feature. You can have main slides and sub slides within those slides. Think of a main slide like a chapter and the sub slide like a subtopic within that chapter.

To create a sub-slide, add a slide (you can add a slide by clicking on the slide in front of it and hitting enter, or by right clicking a slide and click New Slide. Once it's added, move the new slide to the right with your mouse. It will now be indented over from the main slide.

You can do this to as many slides as you want; notice that there's now an arrow on the main slide? Click that and it will collapse it.

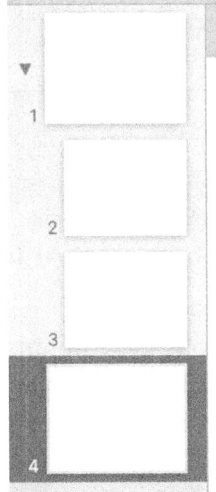

Play Menu

The Play menu is also a little bare, but unlike the slide menu, you'll want to pay close attention to the features if you'll be presenting this presentation somewhere. There are three main features here:

- Play Slideshow – Play will turn your computer into a screen. This is useful if you are presenting from your computer; if you are presenting on a TV or projector, it will look different (which I'll show you below).
- Record Slideshow – Record puts it into presenter mode, so you can narrate the presentation.
- Rehearse Slideshow – Rehearse looks the same as record, but nothing is being recorded; it's in present mode, but it's for practicing only.

Present view looks like the image below; the idea is your presentation will show up as you intend on the TV screen, but on your computer it will look like the presenter's view; here you can preview your next slides, see notes, a timer, etc.—but this is all viewable to you only.

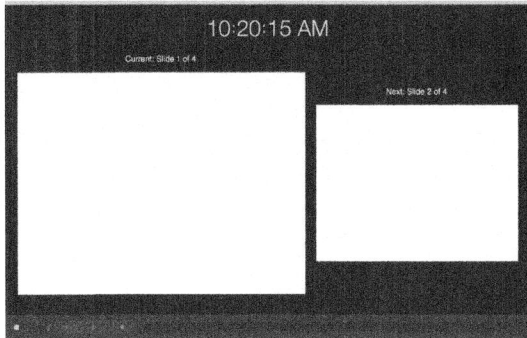

If you go to customize presenter display, you'll see several options for what shows up when you are in this mode.

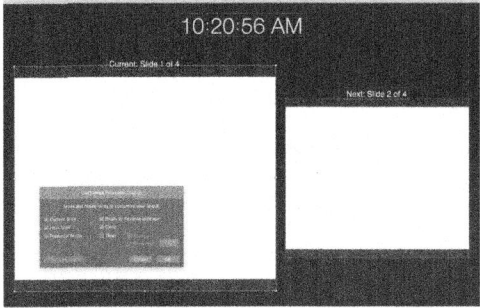

VIEW MENU

The View Menu is where you show and hide menus; we've covered most of the menus, but there's one to note here: Presenter Notes.

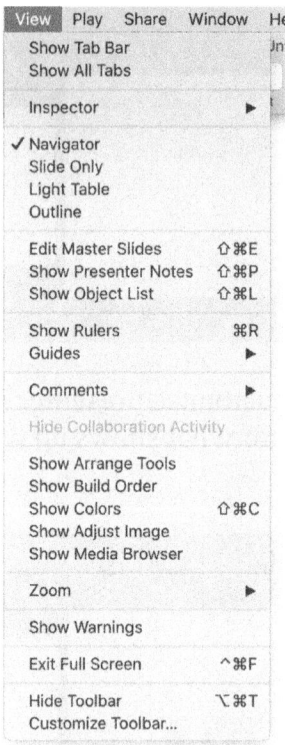

Presenter Notes is where you can add your own comments—such as an outline or even the script for what you intended to say on this slide.

When you present this on a TV, it won't be present to your audience, but you can add it into your presenter mode display.

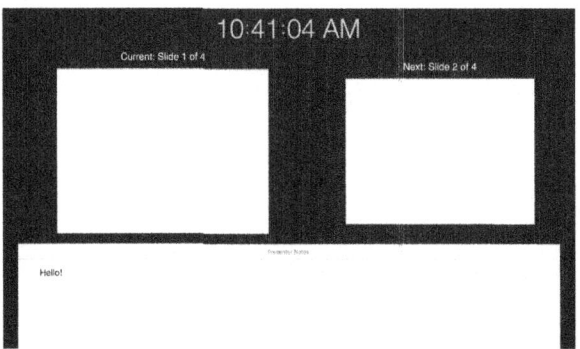

OPENING KEYNOTE FROM ICLOUD

Keynote can be run right from your browser; it's great for editing, but for intensive design work, the best solution will be your computer.

To access it from your browser, head to iCloud.com and sign in with your Apple ID.

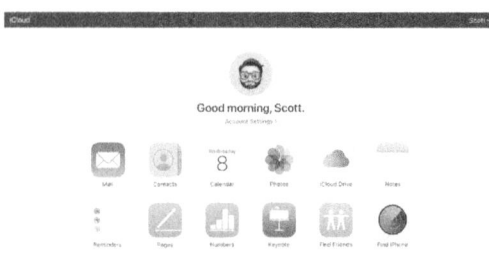

The first screen you'll see will show you all the things you can do from the cloud; one of them is Keynote. Click it once to open it.

As long as you've been saving your work to the cloud, then any recent docs will show up here, and you can click on their thumbnail once to open them.

You can additionally start a new Doc by clicking on the + button in the upper right corner. This will open up Keynote for iCloud. All the features covered in this book can be found in Keynote for iCloud as well.

Managing Documents

Saving in Keynote is pretty straightforward—especially if you've used Windows before. It's under File > Save.

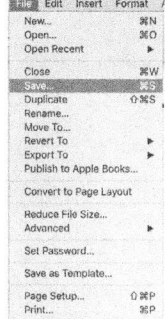

Before we move forward with using other features in Keynote, I want to go over the less straightforward ways to manage documents.

Renaming Documents

Renaming documents is very easy. Like many things in Keynote, there's more than one way to do it.

The easiest way is when your document is open; just click on the name in the top center of the document.

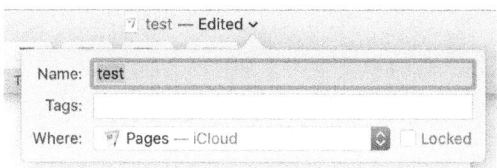

The next way is File > Rename.

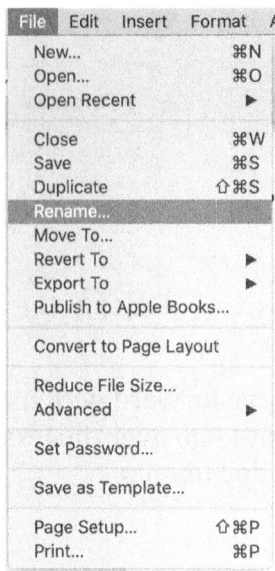

The third way is to find it in Finder, click with two fingers, and select Rename.

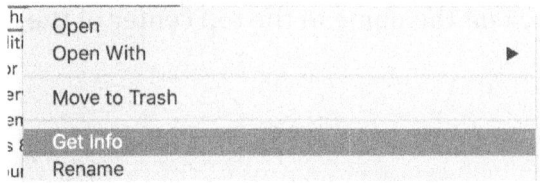

[2]
Photos for Keynote

This chapter will cover:
- Insert image
- Arrange / Rotate / Wrap image
- Edit Mask / Alpha
- Image Styling

As much as possible, I'm trying to make learning Keynote fun; there's no better way to make something fun than with photos!

As we go, we'll be learning more about styling tips, but before we get there, we are going to learn about photos—not just about inserting them into the document, but about how to apply more advanced techniques to them.

Inserting An Image

Inserting an image can be done several ways. You can copy and paste an image into the document; you can drag a photo into the document; or you can pick it manually.

To pick it manually, you can go to Insert > Choose, and then find the file location.

The quicker way to add a photo, however, is from the menu. Click the image button, which shows you all the different types of media types you can add. You can get photos by clicking on Photos or Image Gallery (if the photos are in your gallery) or by clicking "Choose" to pick where the photo is located.

If you pick photos, it's not going to show you all your photos—just the photos in that photos area of your Mac. You could, for example, have a photo on your USB drive. If that's the case, then you'd want to pick "Choose" from the previous menu instead of photos.

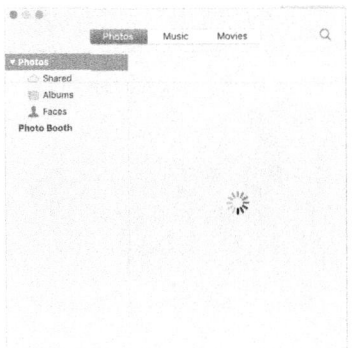

ARRANGING IMAGES

RESIZE AND ROTATE

Once your image is inserted, you can use your mouse to move it, resize it, and rotate it. Resizing is pretty straightforward. Click the image, then move to the corner or side of the image and move the little squares on the edges in and out. To rotate the image you'll do the same thing, but when you get to the corner of the image, press the Command key on your keyboard. This will show you a curved line and also show you the percentage of the rotation as you move the image.

Hint: Looking for images? I often use a website named pexels.com to find public domain (or free to use) images.

There's one more way to rotate an image. When you click on the image, you'll notice that the side panel that you used to format text has changed. It's now a new menu with controls to format an image.

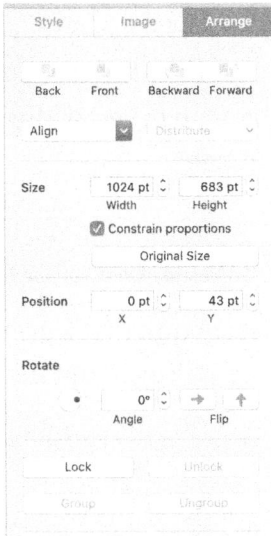

There are three buttons on top of this menu (Style, Image, Arrange); we'll go over the first button in the next section, but for this section, go to Arrange.

On the bottom of this menu, there's a section called Rotate; angle is what you want to use. The mouse is a quick and easy way to rotate your image, but if you want precision, then this is the best method. Next to the Angle, you can also vertically and horizontally flip the image using the arrows.

Placement

Because a photo is essentially just a layer in your slide, you can position it behind or in front of other layers.

If you go to the Arrange menu, you'll notice a bar with icons that say Back / Front.

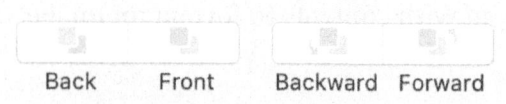

This is where you go to move the image behind or in front of other images.

Image Grouping

There's one last section that's greyed out in Arrange: Grouping. Grouping is greyed out because you need two images to use it.

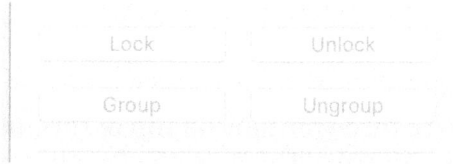

Add a second image, then click one image, press command on your keyboard and select the second image; the Group option is no longer greyed out. What grouping does is put two images together; so when you edit the size, rotation, etc. you are treating the two photos as one image.

If you want to edit just one image, you don't have to ungroup it. You can double click the image to tell Keynote that you want to keep them grouped, but you want to make changes to one photo while they are grouped.

WATERMARKS

There are a few ways to create a Watermark in Keynote; the easiest way is to move the image behind everything and make it a little bit transparent in the Style menu.

What if you want that same image on every slide, however? You can do that by changing the master slides, which I mentioned in the previous chapter.

Edit Mask and Alpha

With your image selected (note: if the images are grouped, you need to double click the image you want to edit—you can't edit both images at the same time), select the Image button.

This brings up options for image enhancements. At the bottom is the Adjustments section; this section is pretty self-explanatory- the Exposure and Saturation sliders will change the amount of exposure / saturation in the image. The Enhance button will do an auto enhancement based on what the computer thinks the image should look like (the reset button will undo it).

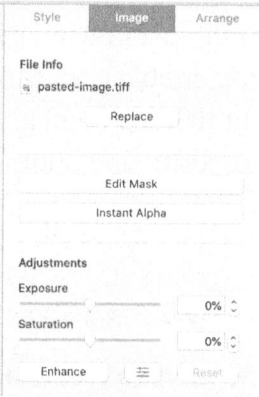

Next to the Enhance button is a control button; this will bring up more adjustment controls.

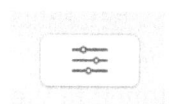

Most people probably won't need this many controls, but it's helpful to know they are there.

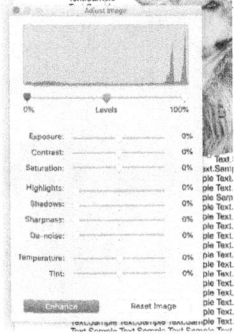

The section that may not be as easy to understand is the top section: Edit Mask and Instant Alpha.

Edit Mask is essentially an image crop. You can use this to cut off parts of the image without resizing it.

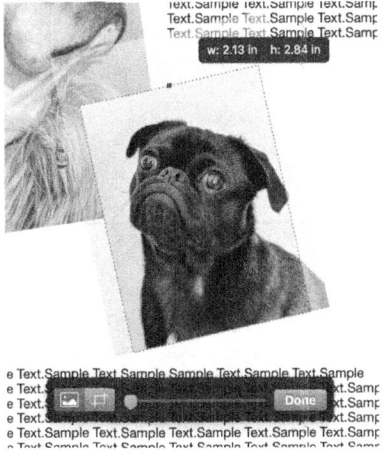

Instant Alpha is one of my personal favorite image editing tools. It removes the background of the image. It's great when your image has a very solid background (you're standing against a solid color wall, for example).

One you click on it, the cursor turns to a square box and you can click and drag over the areas you want to take out.

As you click, the sections that are removed will turn a different color to indicate what has been removed. When you're done, let go of the mouse and click the done button.

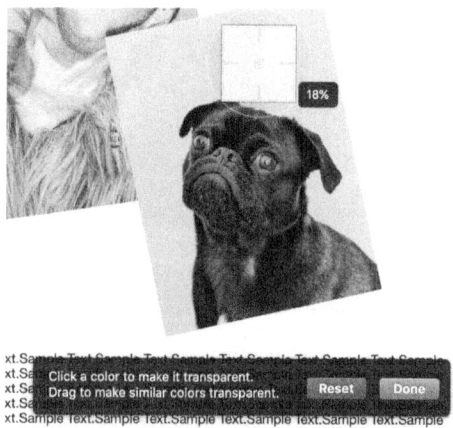

As you remove the background, it is also autocropping; so if you've removed the background from the top, the image has automatically been cropped to accommodate for it.

Styling Your Image

Now that we know how to move an image around, let's add some style to it.

To style your image, tap the image. Style is the first button on the image edit menu.

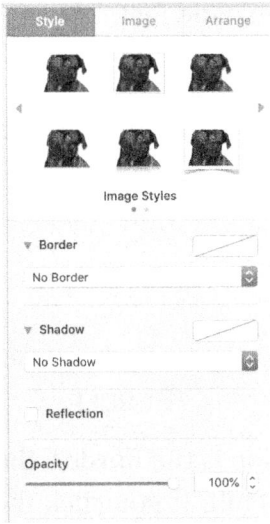

Basic Styles

The top box lets you add quick, pre-defined image styles to your image. For example, if you want your image to have a box around it.

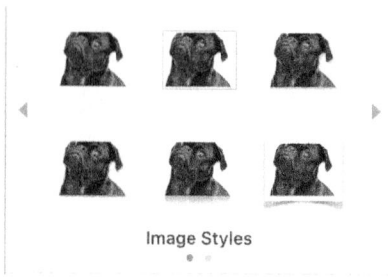

Image Styles

Most people will probably want to do manual editing to the photo, but if you use the arrow in this section, you'll notice a + button. Once you manually make changes to the image (add your transparency, borders, etc.), you can use this button to save these changes so you can apply them to another photo that you want to have a similar look and feel.

Image Styles

Border

The next section is the Border; there is no border on the image by default. If you click the box with the red diagonal line, it will show a drop down of all the different styles.

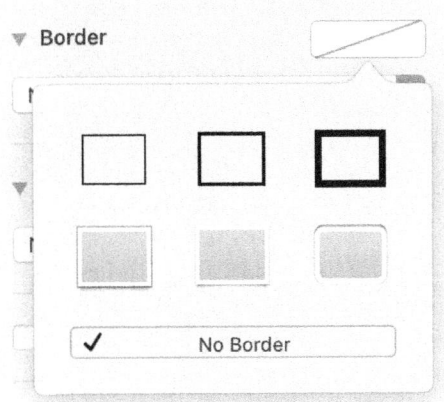

Once you pick your border style, you be able to adjust weight of the border using the slider.

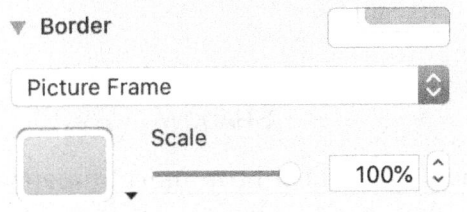

If you click the preview of the border, you will also see all the different border styles for the style that you have picked. Styles vary depending on the style you are using.

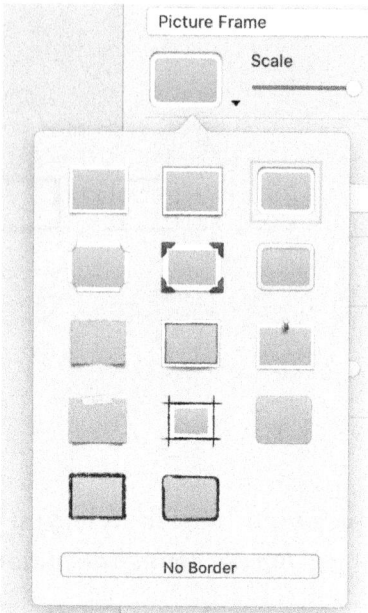

SHADOW

Shadows can add a little more dimension to your photo and help it pop off the page more. It works very similar to Borders; click the thumbnail with the red line through it, then pick the shadow style.

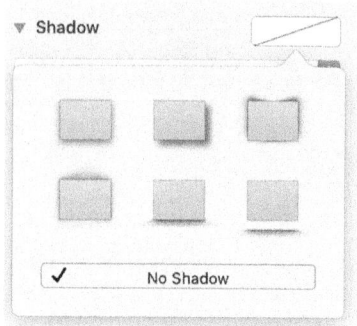

Once you pick the style, you'll get several shadow options to increase or decrease the amount of shadowing used.

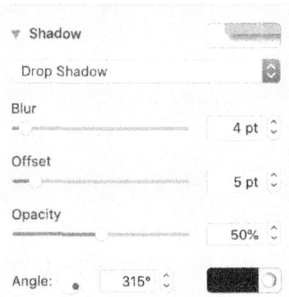

As you make changes, the image will change in real-time, so you will immediately see the effects. Notice in the image below how the image has a more 3D look?

Reflection

Reflection is a simple check / uncheck box; you can use the slider to adjust the amount of reflection used, but that's the only edit available.

You can see in the example below how the reflection gave the image the appearance of an image reflecting on the page (the reflection is the darken area on the bottom of the image).

Transparency

The final style change is transparency. Transparency makes an image more see-through (see the example below). This is great for something like a watermark, but doesn't help a lot if you don't have something below the image.

In the below example, I put the transparent image above another photo to illustrate how you can use it on top of another image.

[3]
Tables

This chapter will cover:
- Inserting a table
- Styling a table
- Deleting a table
- Importing a table

Keynote works seamlessly with other iWork apps like Numbers and Pages; this is especially true with tables. You can insert tables into your document manually, but you can also import tables from Numbers into it. This section will show you how and will also serve as a brief introduction to Numbers for the iPad.

Inserting a Table

If you have ever added a table in Word, then you may be used to picking the size and width before adding the table; in Keynote, you add the table and then adjust it accordingly.

To add a table, tap the Table button from the top menu bar (you can also use Insert > Table from the menu options at the top of MacOS). You'll have several styles to pick from, but, again, this is different from Word where you drag to the number of rows and columns that you want.

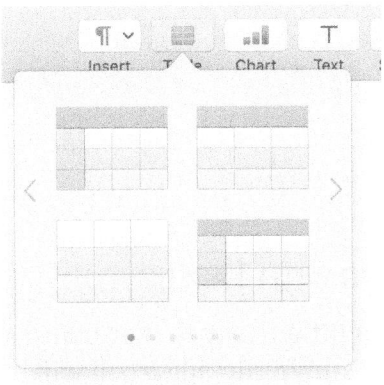

ADDING COLUMNS AND ROWS

Your table is now inserted, but chances are it's not the right size.

At the bottom of the last row (or side of the last column) there's a circle with two lines. Click on either of those to adjust the number of columns / rows. You can either use the up / down arrows to pick, or you can click the number and then type the amount you want.

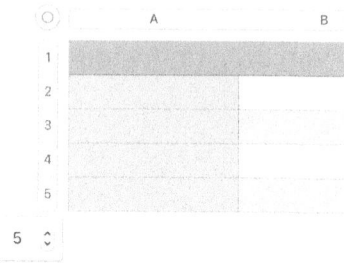

INTERACTING WITH TABLES

It can be a little tricky to work with a table in Keynote at first. Double clicking a cell will bring up the keyboard, but single clicking it will select the entire cell (Microsoft Excel users should have an easier time with this concept).

If there's no text you can single click and start typing, but if you want to edit the text that's already there, there you need to double click.

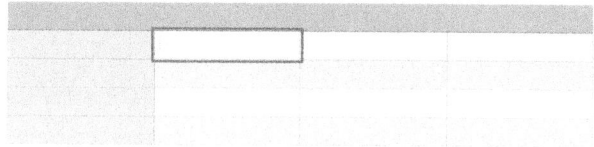

Row / Column Options

If you want to delete or add a row / column, then go to the row or column you want to make changes to, and then click the drop-down arrow. Several options will come up.

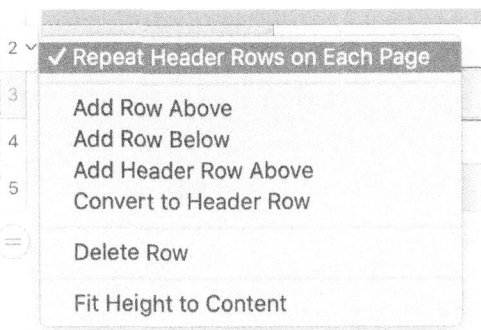

You can also click the number associated with the row / column to select all. This is helpful if you want to copy / paste a row or column.

Styling Tables

Apple's predefined tables look great, but if you've got a specific color scheme or style in mind, it's easy to customize your tables to match that. Just select your table (or certain cells in your table) and look to the right-side menu, which has changed to a table-style menu.

Table Options

The first set of options is for the entire table.

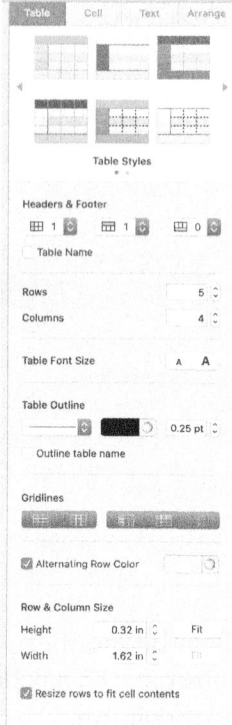

These are all options that would change everything in the table. Such as the table outline, for example if you want, you can see grids and alternating row colors (if you want row 1 white, row 2 black, row 3 white, row 4 black, etc.). You can also increase the font size and add new rows and columns.

The Table Styles at the top are similar to the image styles; they're predefined styles.

CELL OPTIONS

The table options are great if you want to change everything about the table. But what if you just want to change a cell, column, or row? That's where the Cell Option tab comes into play.

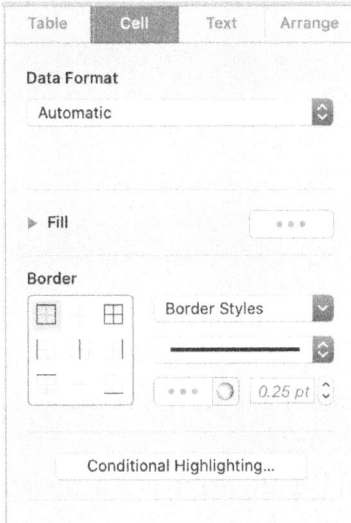

It says "Cell" but Cell here is anything that you highlight. So if you highlight one cell, then it's just that cell; but if you highlight multiple cells, then it's each of those cells.

Data Format is where you can change what is inside the cell; what does that mean? Let's say one of your columns had only currency; you could highlight that column and then say that everything in those cells was currency, so a dollar sign would be added to all the numbers in the cells.

58 | *The Ridiculously Simple Guide to Keynote For Mac*

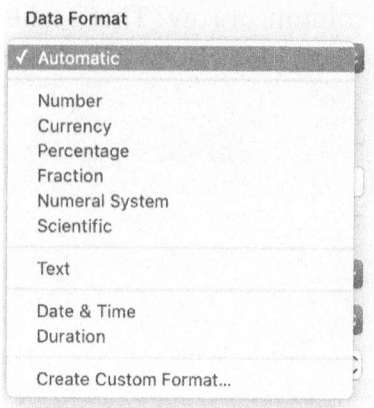

You can change the color of the cell under Fill; you can change the border style, border color, and border weight under Border.

Conditional Highlighting is a little less obvious that those first couple of options.

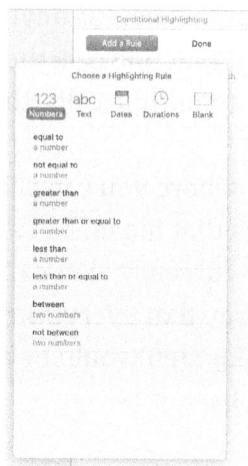

This lets you create rules; for example anytime you have a cell with the number 2, the cell text turns Bold.

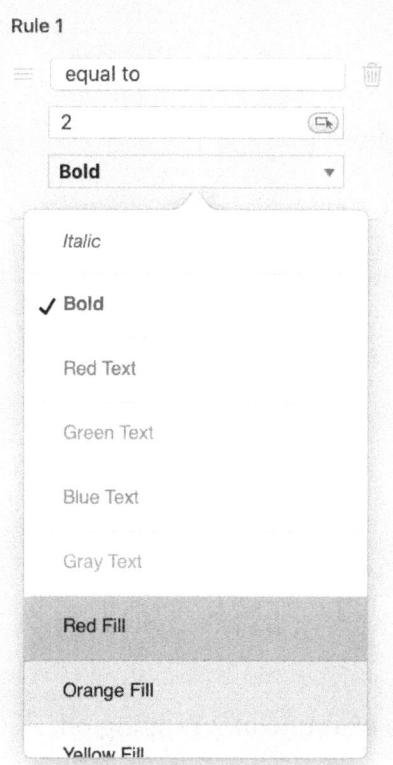

TEXT OPTIONS

By now you should understand how to format text. It's no different when you are doing a table. The same rules as before apply—any cell you highlight will have the text changed—so if you have the entire row highlighted, then all the text in those cells changes.

There is one box worth noting: Wrap text in cell. It's just a check / uncheck box, but it's important because if you have a long string of text and you want it to fit within a cell without going into the next cell, then you need it to wrap.

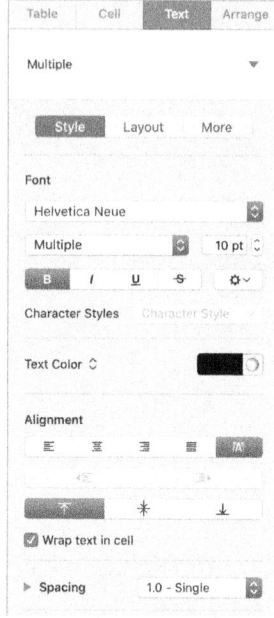

Here's an example of wrapping off.

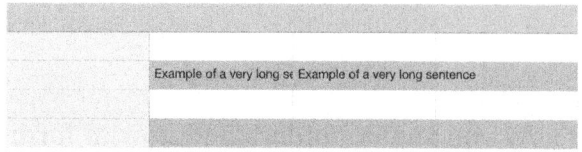

And here's what it looks like on.

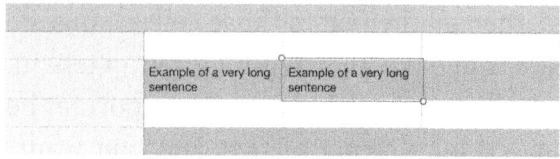

ARRANGE OPTIONS

Just like text options are the same as formatting options outside of the table, Arrange Options are almost identical that the options covered in Photo Arrangement options.

DELETING TABLES

Deleting an entire table is a quick process. Click the table. Hit delete.

Importing Tables

Importing a table from somewhere else can be done a few different ways.

The first, and quickest, way is to copy and paste the table. Command V is obviously the easiest way to do this, but go to the Edit menu. Notice there's a Paste and a Paste and Match Styles? If you aren't getting the paste results that you want, try this Paste instead.

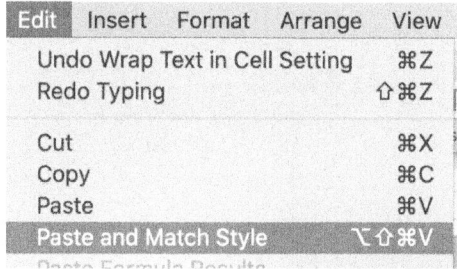

If you don't need to make changes to the table, what a lot of people prefer to do is just make a screenshot of the spreadsheet: Command + Shift + 3 (or Command + Shift + 4 if you want to do only select areas of the screen).

[4]
CHARTS

This chapter will cover:
- Inserting a Chart
- Editing Chart Data
- Styling a Chart

Charts can add color and interest to your documents, as well as help you present data more clearly. Keynote includes a powerful Charts feature that allows you to quickly create beautiful, customizable charts that really pop out of the page.

Now that you know how to use Tables, using Charts will be a breeze.

INSERTING A CHART

To insert a chart in Keynote, tap the Insert button, then tap Charts. From here, you'll choose the type of chart (bar, area, line, pie), as well as the style you want. Choose from several different color schemes in 2D, 3D, and interactive. If you change your mind about your chart choice, you can always change it later, without losing any data you've entered. Just tap on your favorite chart to insert it into your document.

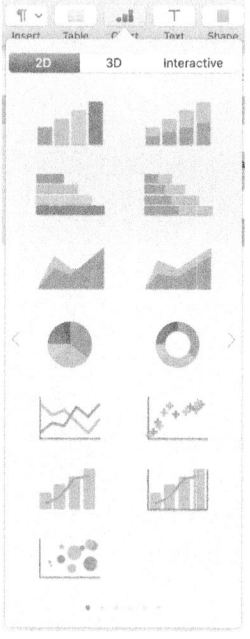

As with almost everything in Keynote, you can also add Charts from the top menu (Insert > Chart).

Scott La Counte | 65

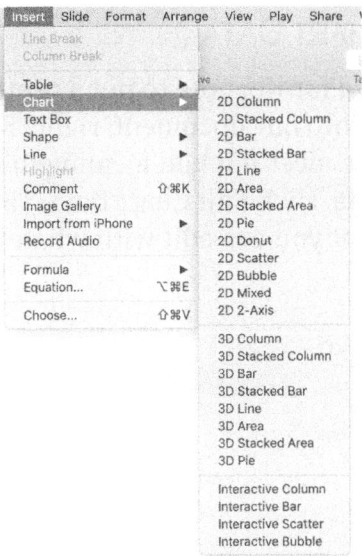

Once you have your chart picked, a chart that's already filled out will be added to your document (I'm using a Pie chart in this chapter, but the same features apply to almost all of the charts—they just look a little different).

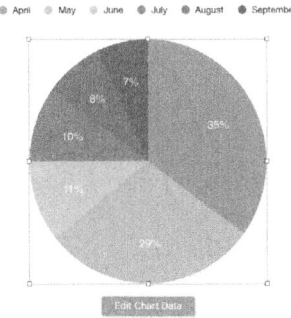

Editing Chart Data

It's so nice for Keynote to put a pretty chart that's all filled out into our document, right? Sure! But wouldn't it be nicer if it had meaningful data? To add your own data, click Edit Chart Data. This brings up a mini table that you can edit with whatever information you want.

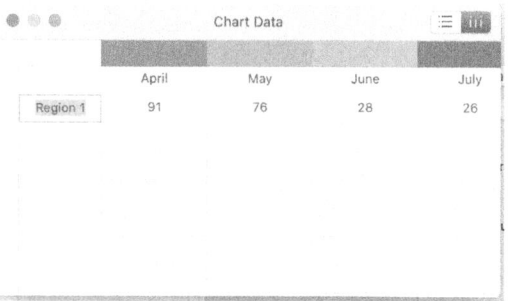

I'm going to replace the months with the names of states, and use an entirely different data range. The chart changes with each change I make in the table. Notice the chart below is completely different from the one above?

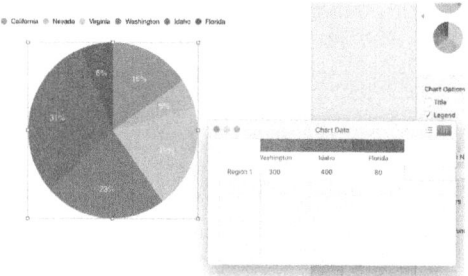

You can enter additional rows if you need to—but this won't work on all charts (like the pie chart).

STYLING YOUR PIE CHART

Now that you have the data you want, it's time to style it.

If you did a pie chart, then you'll see three options on the side (Chart, Wedges, Arrange).

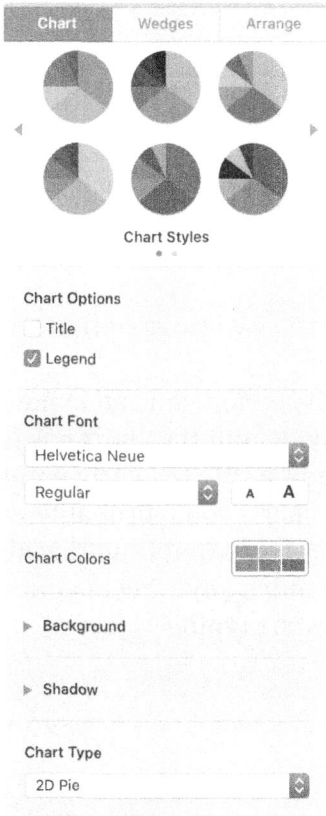

Other charts (like bar charts) have four (Chart, Axis, Series, Arrange).

I'll go over the two extra options for a bar chart in the next section.

In the Chart section you can make changes to the entire chart. By default the chart has no title, but if you check off the box, a title (cleverly named "Title") is added to your chart; you'll probably want to name it something else. To do that (and this also applies to re-naming pretty much anything in your chart) double click on it and start typing.

Below the title is where you can change the font; and under that, the chart colors. When you click on the chart colors, it gives you a whole host of pre-defined colors. But what if you want to pick your own?

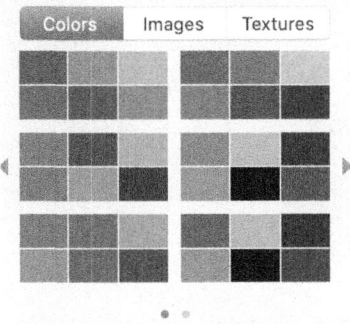

There's one extra small step to pick your own colors. You have to double click on the wedge that you want to change the color of, and then over on the menu options to the right of it, click Style (Style is a new option that's only there if you double click the wedge). From here, you can pick a color under "Fill."

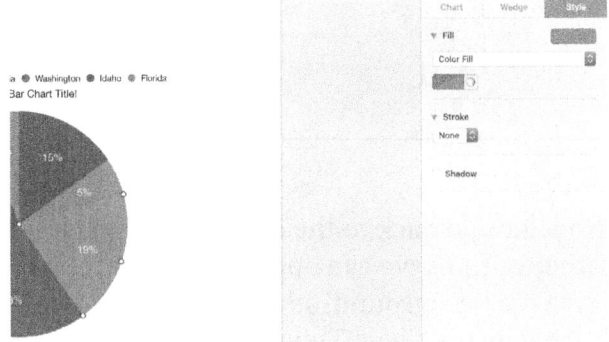

While we are in this section, let's go just under it to Stroke and Shadow. Both of these options help a wedge stand out a little. This is useful if you want to illustrate one area of the chart of others. See in the example below how I added a dotted line (and increased the line weight to 4) and also added a shadow.

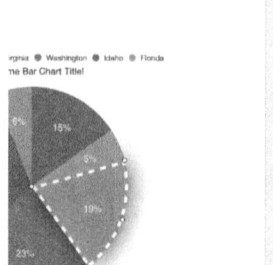 

If you really want that wedge to stand out, try pulling it apart from the chart. You can do that by clicking on the Wedge option, and then changing the Wedge Position. Look at the example below; the wedge is now separated in the chart.

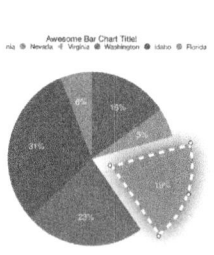 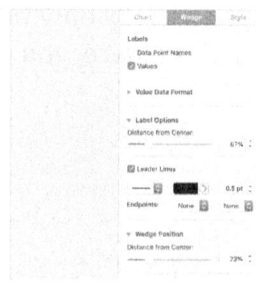

Now let's go back to the chart section and look at the other options we can apply to the entire chart. You can give it a background, add a shadow to it, and finally, change the Chart Type. You can make it a different Pie chart or turn it into a line chart (note: this will probably interfere with your data and you may have to redo some of it).

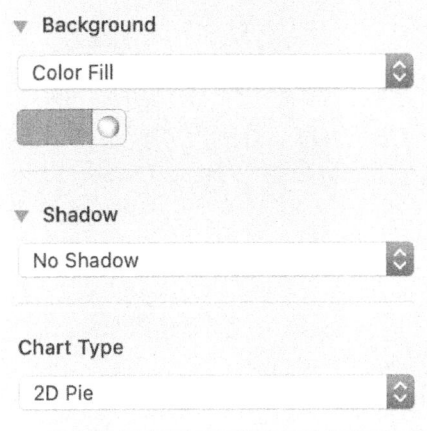

We saw how going to the Wedge section could separate your single wedge from the rest. If you don't double click the wedge and change it, below is what happens.

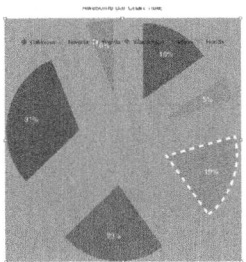

All the wedges separate. If that's what you want, then perfect! If that's not what you want, undo and then double click the wedge you want to separate.

Checking off Data Point Names will put the names of the value in the chart (you can also keep it in the Legend).

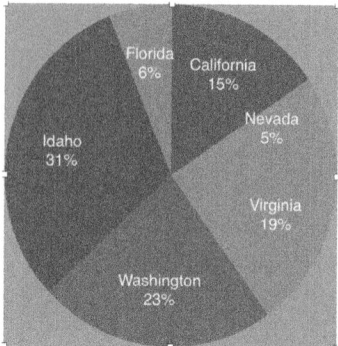

The values on the chart are currently showing as a percentage; if you prefer showing them as a number (or another value type), you can change this under Value Format.

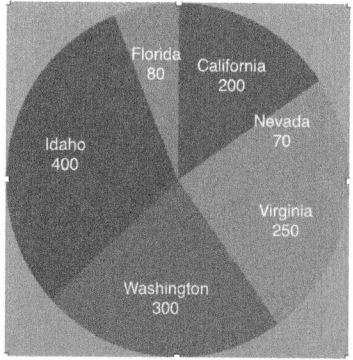

If you check off Lender Lines, you probably won't notice a difference; to see what the lines are, click the Straight drop-down and change it to Angled.

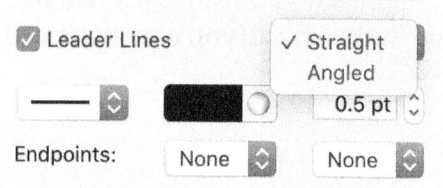

You should now see lines to the side of the chart.

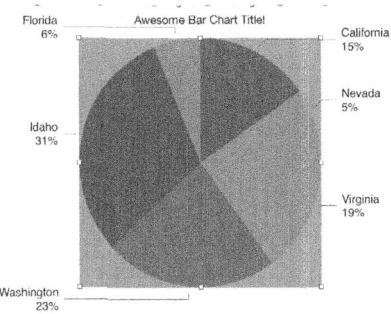

The arrange option should look familiar to you. You've seen it in the Tables section and the Photos section; it's the same features.

STYLING YOUR BAR CHART

Now that you know how to style a Pie Chart, you'll have no problem with the Bar Chart; it's basically the same, but with more options for labels.

In the axis sub-tab, you can turn category labels, series names, gridlines and titles on and off. Similarly, in the Y-axis or X-axis sub-tab, you can turn value labels, gridlines and titles on and off. Here you can also specify the number format you'd like to use and adjust the value scale settings. Number formatting includes the option to add prefixes and suffixes, like currency symbols or suffixes like %, millions, etc.

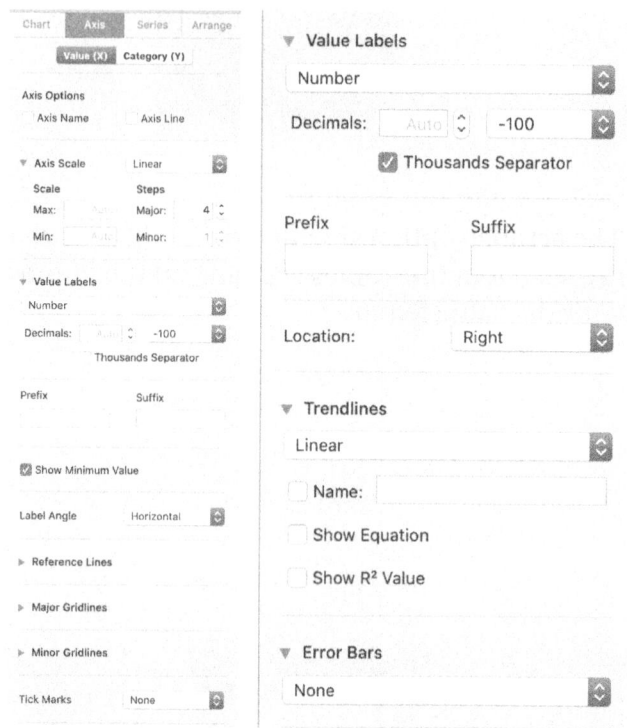

Note: the contents of the sub-tabs change depending on the orientation of your chart. The number formatting option may appear under either the x- or y-axis, depending on the type of chart you've inserted.

[5]
SHAPES

> This chapter will cover:
> - Inserting a Shape
> - Resizing Shapes
> - Creating Text Boxes

Pictures are great! They really help your document look snazzy. But there's one more type of graphical illustration you should consider: shapes. Shapes can be great additions to a document – they can be used to draw attention to an area of a document or to illustrate your points graphically. Keynote offers a number of handy pre-made shapes for you to use, and I'll show you how to get the most out of them.

INSERTING A SHAPE

To insert a shape into a document, click the shape button or go to Insert > Shape from the top menu. This will bring up all of the shapes available for you. Find the one you like and click it to insert it.

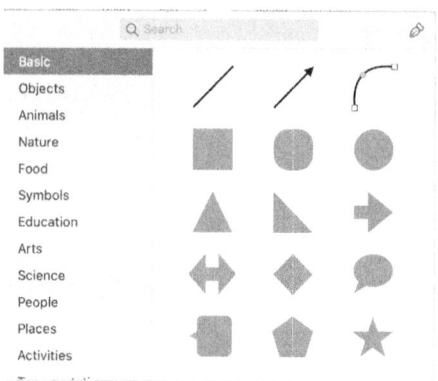

Remember that you can change the color, border and shadow/reflection effects later!

Shapes sounds a little misleading. If you're like me, you're probably thinking square, circle, etc. But shapes in Keynote are kind of like clipart. Yes, basic shapes are there, but so are other things. In the example below I searched for "Dog" and got five results.

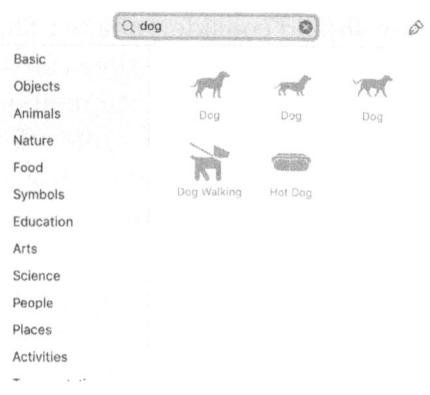

Resizing Shapes and Adjusting Proportions

Shape resizing is just like resizing photos: tap on a corner and drag it to the desired size. However, with Shapes, you can also adjust proportions. What does that mean? It's better shown than explained. Double tap your trackpad on the shape to bring up the shape options. Now click "Make Editable."

There are now a bunch of dots on the shape. These represent points that you can adjust.

As an example, I moved the point inward from the dog's stomach and look what happened.

By default, you make these changes with a curved point, but you can change this by bringing the options up again. Notice the three different points?

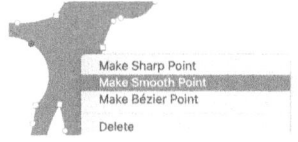

Moving and Rotating Shapes

To move a shape, simply tap on it and drag it to a new location. To rotate a shape, click image then press the command button—just like you would an image.

Adding Text to a Shape

To add text on top of a shape, double-tap on it to activate its text field. Then just type your text!

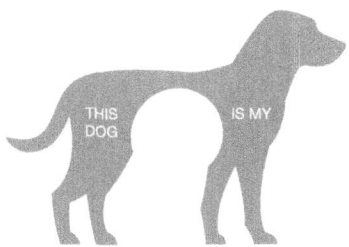

CREATING TEXT BOXES

There's one more type of shape, but it's not under shape. It's a Text Box. Text Boxes are exactly what they sound like—floating boxes that have text.

Why use Text Box instead of typing out the text? Ideally, you want to use them when you are making something like a title—not when you are typing out your epic novel. It's for short text that you want to stand out.

Unlike standard text, Text Boxes are treated in the same way images are, so you can easily move them around and have other things wrap around them.

To get started, click the T in the menu.

You can also do Insert > Text Box.

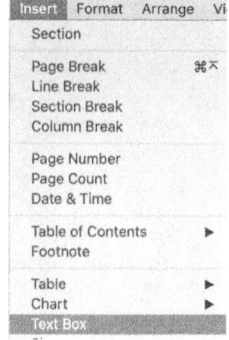

This puts a floating box with generic text in your document.

You can change the color of the box and more by clicking on Style; it has all the same types of options that you'd find in the Image or Shape options.

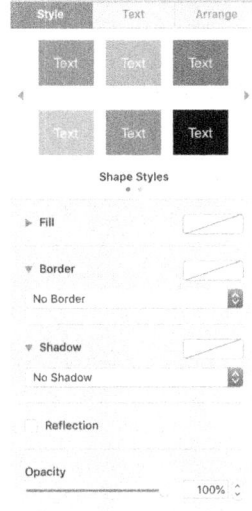

Because it's a Shape, you are able to edit it like you would a shape. In the below example, I curved out the bottom portion of the box.

STYLING SHAPES AND TEXT BOXES

Styling Shapes and Text boxes is the same as styling an image, so I won't repeat myself here. If you are confused about styling, refer to the section in the Photos chapter.

[6]
TEMPLATES

This chapter will cover:
- Using third-part Keynote Templates
- Creating your own Templates

Keynote comes with several templates. What exactly is a Template? A Template is a document that's already formatted—complete with text and images. Why would you want that? The idea is you delete the text (and replace the images) to make it your own, but save time on the sometimes complicated formatting aspect of it.

Using Third-Party Keynote Templates

The templates in Keynote are nice, but if you use it long enough, you probably will want a few more; if you get to that place, there are websites (and even apps), which sell Keynote templates (sometimes they are free). A basically web search for "Keynote templates" or even "free Keynote templates" will show you what I mean.

Word of caution: like anything you download, use at your own risk. If a website looks sketchy, be wary of downloading a template.

To use a template like this, just go to the website, find a template you like, follow the site's instructions to download it to your computer's hard drive, and then sync it with your iPad as if it were any other Keynote document, using the iTunes File Sharing syncing process discussed in "Basic Features."

After that, Keynote can open the template and you can begin to edit it. It is strongly recommended to make a duplicate of your template document before you begin working on it, so that you will continue to have a blank one for later if you need it.

These third party templates are great for more variety—for example, if you are looking to give your resume a little more creativity.

Creating Your Own "Templates"

Unfortunately, Keynote currently does not allow you to save templates in the Create New Document screen. However, you can work around this sorely missed feature by setting up your "template" as a regular Keynote document.

Personally, I make a duplicate of the document (i.e. File > Duplicate) and name it something like "Resume Template."

[7]
Sharing and Exporting Document

This chapter will cover:
- Sharing your presentation

In spite of the popularity of iPhones and iPads, Apple users still often find themselves marooned in a Windows-based world. Keynote is a wonderful program, but it's incomprehensible to Microsoft PowerPoint. Fortunately, Keynote offers several methods for sharing and exporting Keynote documents in multiple formats. Keynote also makes moving documents across Apple devices absolutely effortless, thanks to iCloud.

Syncing Documents with iCloud

If you've enabled iCloud in your Keynote app, your documents will be synced across your devices automatically with absolutely no work required on your part. You can even access your documents online from any internet connection at www.icloud.com.

Emailing a Document From Keynote

E-mailing documents is one of the most straightforward methods of sharing your document. Go to Share > Send a Copy.

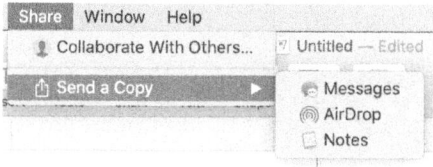

Collaborating

You can also collaborate on a document by going to Share > Collaborate With Others.

This brings up an option that asks how you would like the share the document.

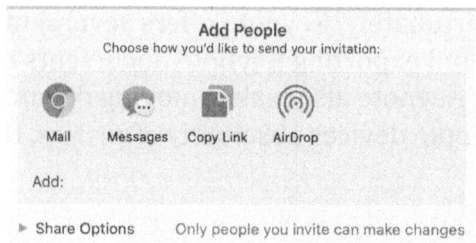

I recommend clicking on the Share Options drop down to make sure the right permissions are enabled. For example, you can make the document readable to anyone you share it with or anyone who gets the document; you can also give the user permission to make changes.

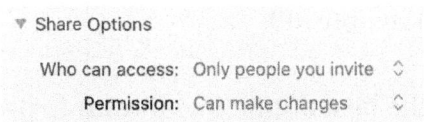

Export a Keynote Document

By default, you'll be saving your file as a .Keynote document. That's great if you have Keynote, but if you're sharing it (or opening it) on a computer that doesn't have Keynote—or you want to create a universal PDF that anyone can see- then you'll need to export it.

This is pretty straightforward. Go to File > Export.

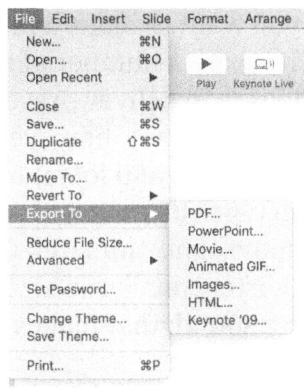

There are seven different file types:

- PDF
- PowerPoint
- Movie
- Animated GIF
- Images
- HTML
- Keynote '09

PDF is the best option if you want to preserve all the formatting in the document and make it look exactly as it appears in Keynote.

Movie and Animated GIF are good if you are sticking it somewhere like a website and you are letting it present itself—in other words, the slides progress without you clicking. Images will export each slide as an Image. And HTML turns your presentation into a website of sorts.

Exporting a Movie

Why would you want to make a movie out of your presentation? There are a number of reasons people do this; the obvious is to deliver presentations without a speaker. Exporting a movie, however, can be used for digital signage, webpages and lots more.

There are two types of moving presentations that you can export: movie and animated GIF. An animated GIF is typically shorter, smaller in size (and resolution), doesn't have sound; that makes it great for websites.

Depending on what you export, you'll have a couple of different options.

For movies, it will ask if it will play automatically, what slides will be in it (All slides is the default), and how long between slides and builds (i.e. the elements you have added - like images and text boxes—assuming you have transitions applied to them); the last option is the resolution.

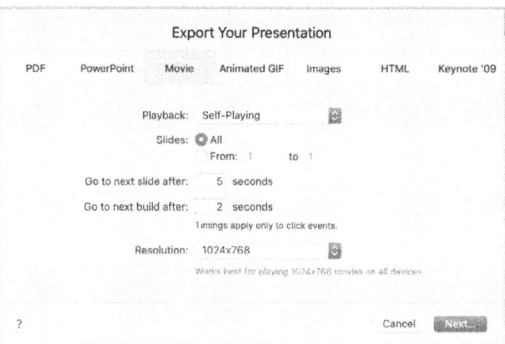

For animated GIFs it will ask what slides, the resolution, and the Frame rate (more frame rate will typically increase your file size).

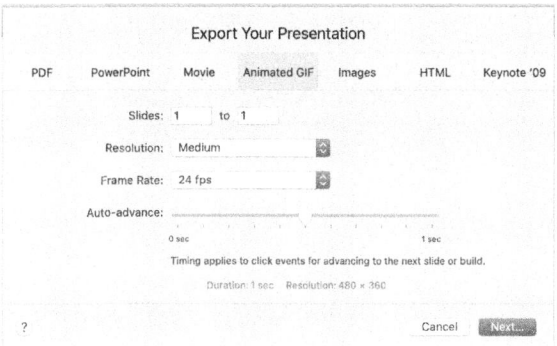

Printing

To print a document, go to File > Print.

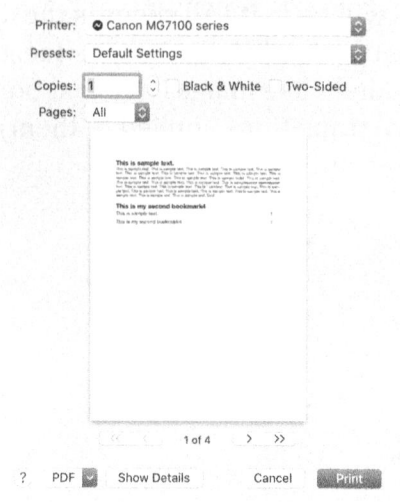

At the bottom of the print menu, there's also an option to save as a PDF. It's Keynote's version of Print to File.

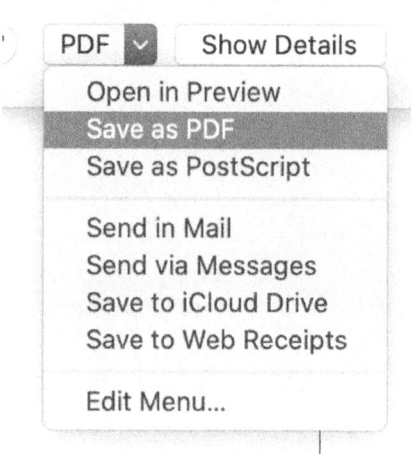

THE WINNING KEYNOTE PITCH DECK

Note: The following Bonus section is taken from my book "Starting Up" which details my experience creating a tech company with limited tech experience; the deck used in this section secured an investment from a multi-billion dollar corporation.

Introduction

You're a young company. You have an idea. You have a dream. Your pitch deck can make or break you! As someone who has successfully raised capital from a multi-billion dollar corporation, you can trust me when I tell you this: your pitch deck is not something you want to mess around with. A huge percent of the time you invest in putting your business together should be spent on your pitch.

My experience with pitching came as part of a startup accelerator. In the program, seven teams went through an intensive business bootcamp where we fine-tuned our businesses and talked to investors. At the end of the program, you pitched your business and hoped someone would make you an offer to invest in your company.

There were great companies in the program. In my opinion, all were worthy of an investment. But you know how many got it? Just my team.

There's a number of things that went into this, and everything wasn't completely centered around the pitch. But the pitch played a big part of it.

So how do you create a pitch-perfect pitch? Let's get started.

POWERPOINT OR KEYNOTE

The first thing you need to tackle is deciding if you are going to use PowerPoint or Keynote. This book is going to cover Keynote because in the pitch world, in my opinion, Keynote is best. Why? For one, it has the best integration to iPad and iPhone. I have made presentations on both devices. A startup founder needs to be able to pitch anywhere, anytime. Can you show PowerPoint on these devices? Yes. But it isn't made for those devices, and I've found it to be a bit cumbersome.

The second reason I like Keynote is it has more emphasis on aesthetics and design. PowerPoint feels like something old me and a stuffy corporation would use.

Getting Started: The Four Key Points to Remember

In this short book, I'll be walking you through my presentation so you can see how to do it right. A few key ingredients before I get to that:

1. **Less is more** - An investor isn't looking for someone who is a bit of a Keynote guru. They aren't going to be more likely to invest if you blow them away with a fancy graphic. In fact, more often than not, it's the opposite. You want what's on the screen to resonate with them. If they're so busy thinking "that's a cool graphic" then they might miss the point you are making with it.
2. **Design simply** - Piggy backing off the last point: let your slides complement what you're saying and not the other way around. For example, you might make a point about a statistic: 100 people. Then the slide would have that number up to reinforce that point.
3. **Brand** - Every slide should have a similar look and feel. Personally, I'm a big fan of

having your logo on the bottom center of the presentation; it keeps your name fresh in the investor's mind.
4. **Your ask** - Don't be vague. Be absolutely clear that you know exactly what it will take to run your business, and have a slide to illustrate it. If you end the presentation and the investor says, "Your asking for 500k. What could you do with 100k?" You darn well better be able to answer it. With "some" companies in the program with me, the ask was the most challenging part. They had absolutely no idea what they would use money on and it showed. They needed money, but they couldn't adequately show why they needed money.

The most important thing to remember about any pitch is this: the investor is betting on you, not the business. If you are an investor and have millions at your disposal, then you could go with any idea pitched to you and do it yourself. They are looking for innovating ideas, but that's secondary to innovating leaders. They're looking for confidence and know-how. They're looking for someone who can get it done.

The Winning Pitch

I'm going to walk you through our pitch next. Here's a high-level overview of the company:

> We were a marketing CMS for self-published writers. We helped writers manage all of their social networks, discover who was talking about them, and generate content ideas for their website.

Our first slide was pretty simple. It had just our logo and three power words to describe us. If you don't have power words for your startup, then start brainstorming and make them! If you can't think of just three words to describe what you do, then you're not a business yet. You're a napkin idea that's not ready for funding.

The next two slides set up a problem in the publishing industry. It showed successful writers; writers that would resonate with the audience (who were publishing experts) because they had each sold over 1,000,000 books. These are all the darlings of the self-publishing world and the writers that every writer "thinks" they can be.

The colors on these slides match the companies branding. And each slide has the company's logo.

The next four slides show the problem that has been setup: it sucks to be a self-published writer.

Be shocking here. Make your audience really feel the pain of your end user.

In our case, this is what we showed:

Of the 3,000,000 self-published books that come out every year, only 40 writers have ever sold more than 1,000,000 books. The odds of a writer doing it: 0.001333% To make it stick a little more, I explained that was about the same odds as getting struck by lightning.

You have to know what your audience is thinking. At this point, I knew they'd be thinking "well, yeah, only a few have sold a million, but that doesn't mean you can't make a living at this." And so I pulled it back even further to clarify the average author only sells 150 copies a year. That comes out to less than $500. $500 for all those months of hard work. That stinks, right?

What if there were a way to help them?!

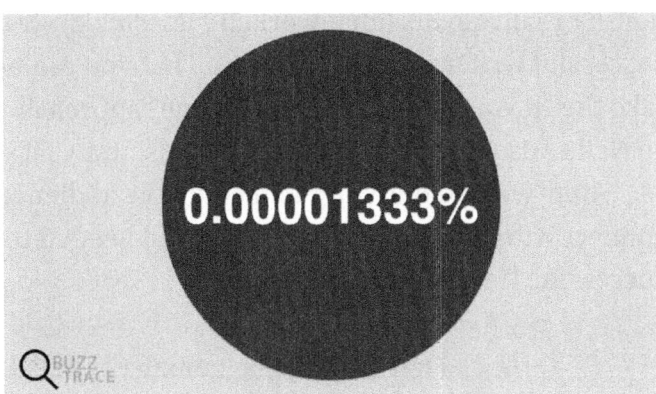

Average Number of Copies Sold Per Year

Less Than 150

Next, I introduced my character. All pitches need to have some kind of narrative. Investors need to hear a story. And these next slides were our story.

Our story is about Neil. Neil is your average writer. He has a job, but he dreams of writing books—sci-fi books in his case. And so he spends the next year skipping out on his friends so he can do what he's always dreamed: write a novel.

Unfortunately, Neil is like most writers and doesn't really do his homework. He doesn't know that successful writers need a platform. That you can't just take the "if you write it, they will come" approach. And so Neil ends up selling just 93 books his first year!

After we told our story and made the audience connect with Neil, we showed what Neil needed to be successful. He needed three things:

1. Social network management
2. Analytics & tools
3. A roadmap for success

And I should clarify here that we didn't just make up Neil's story. Neil was the composite of over 200 user interviews.

Before you get to this point in your deck, make sure you have talked to at least 100 users to validate your idea. And don't wait for them to come to you. When I was in the startup program, I heard from one guy who said, "they aren't giving us users to interview!" And I basically told him to go cry a river! Don't expect anyone to hand you users: find them! I spent hours on discussion boards asking for volunteers. They were pretty easy to find because we were building them something that they needed. If you want an investment, then you need drive and hustle. If you don't have the energy to find users, then maybe you need to rethink your career path.

The next two slides covered competition.

I hear about a lot of startups who think they are doing something original. They don't have competition because they are the first to do it. Bull! Everyone has competition. Everyone.

Your competition doesn't have to be direct, or even an obvious competitor. If you're struggling, then think like this: where do your potential customers currently go to solve their problem?

When Uber started, they didn't have a direct competitor. Their competitors were taxis, public transportation, and friends who gave you a lift to wherever you were going. You may have had to think outside the box.

So in our case, I laid out where people typically went for help and what made us different. And then I showed our biggest selling point: we were one platform that solved all a writer's problems, and we were built for writers.

Competitive Landscape

	Social Management	Analytics / Tools	Roadmap	Cost	Industry Specific
BUZZ TRACE	O	O	O	$	O
Publicist / Marketers			O	$$$$	O
mention	O	O		$	
	O	O		$	
AuthorCheckpoint		O		$	O

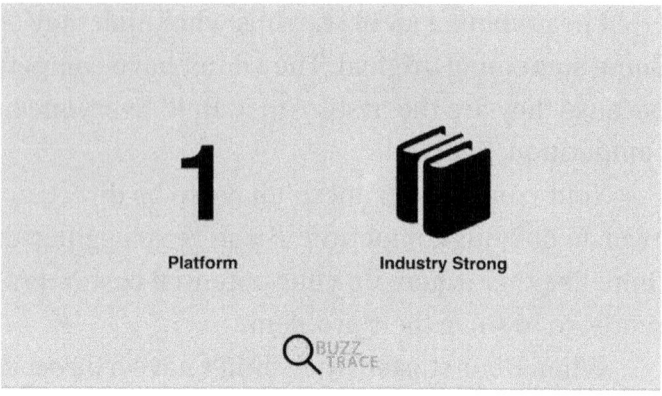

Now it was time to show off what we wanted to do. The next several slides was a prototype of the software. It was design only because we had not finished development. But it should give you some encouragement because it's proof that investors aren't necessarily looking for something ready for market.

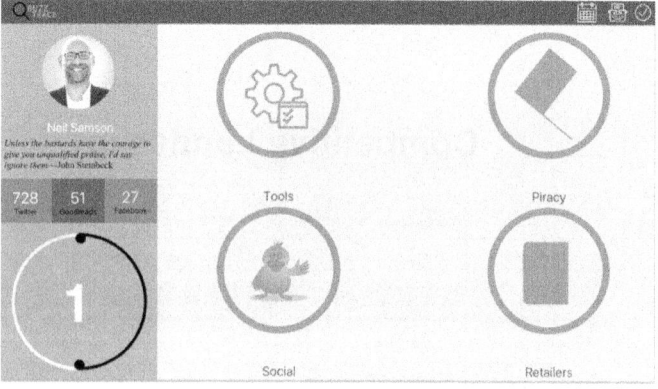

To give the impression that this worked, each slide made it appear that I clicked on something resulting in an action. Even though there were only twenty slides, this portion of the presentation took only a few minutes. It didn't feel that lengthy to the audience because they didn't see everything in the backend of the presentation.

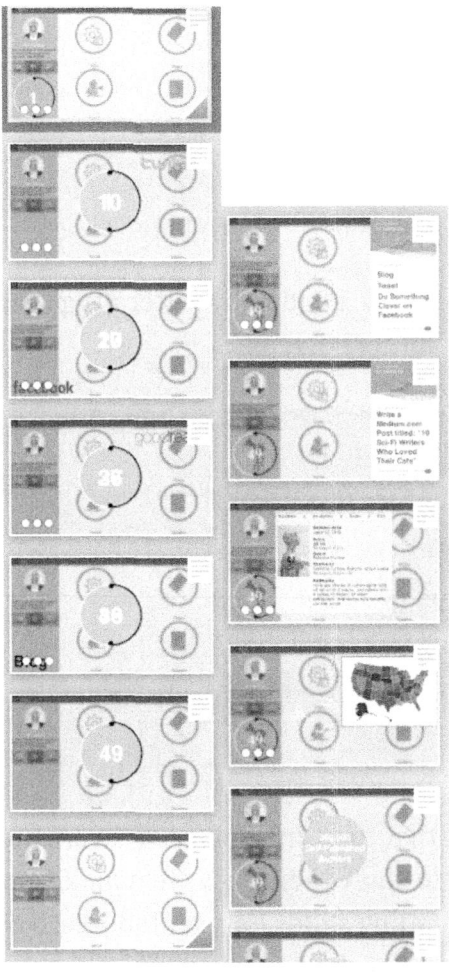

I used a black and white blur effect so the feature I was talking about was in color, but everything else was blurred out.

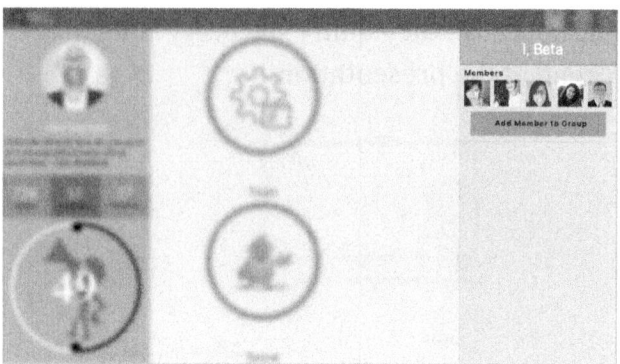

And finally, I ended by reiterating that this solves all of the author's needs.

Now that they knew what we were doing, my next goal was to show them how we'd make money.

The ending slides I presented relatively quickly. Investors will ask questions about these numbers after. Focus your pitch on a problem and how you are solving it. They're concerned about their money, so trust me, they'll ask you questions if you cover something too quickly. The most important thing is you are ready to answer them.

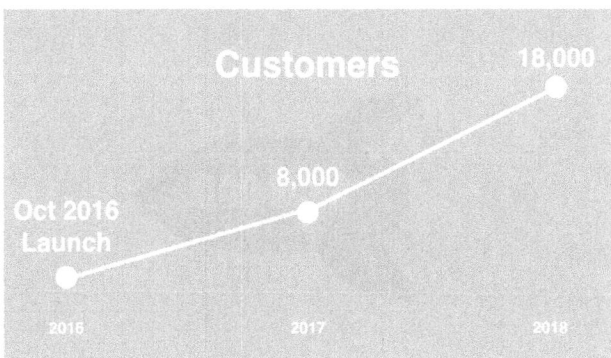

Once they are hopefully hooked, then you get to the moment we've all been waiting for: The ask.

I can't stress this enough: know to a T what you will spend money on! Don't say you need a million dollars if you have no way to justify it. And don't say you need $100,000 because that's how much you make in you current job and you just need to earn what you make!

Our ask was very simple:

- We needed $350k
- That money would get us to 18,000 customers
- And then I categorized where it would go

This was very high-level, but, again, I was absolutely prepared to go into it in more detail after the presentation. And the question did come up—both in the follow-up conversation after the pitch and during the follow-up calls after that.

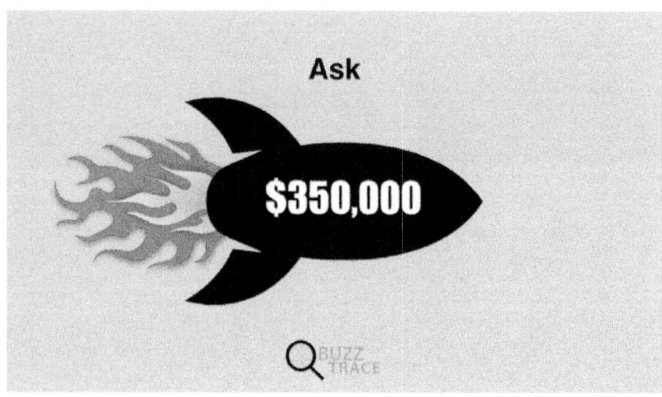

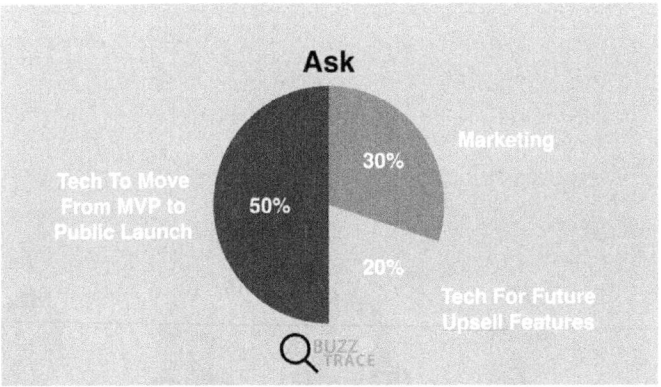

Now that we've had our ask, why us? Why are we the leaders they want to bet on? This is where you sell your experience. There's an old phrase in the startup world: bet on the jockey (the founder) not the horse (the idea). This is where you sell yourself as the jockey.

For these slides, I quickly covered what we had done in the publishing industry amongst ourselves.

Finally, I ended with a contact slide. That slide is important! That's what will be on the screen while you are answering questions. Make sure you have a way for potential investors to contact you. Some may leave early and will jot down your contact information as you are answering questions for others.

Contact

Scott La Counte

scott@buzztrace.com

www.BuzzTrace.com

Conclusion

That's it. That's what got us an investment. Hopefully you saw how simple works, that if you aren't some crazy, creative designer, that's okay. In fact, it's actually quite perfect.

While learning to pitch, I looked at hundreds of winning decks and 95% of them were ridiculously simple. Simple sells!

If you are interested in knowing more about how to raise money for your idea, check out my short book "Starting Up." Or find out more about how to design your idea in "The Ridiculously Simple Guide to Sketch App."

Appendix: Keyboard Shortcuts

General Keyboard Shortcuts

Action	Shortcut
Close a window	Command-W
Close all windows	Option-Command-W
Duplicate a document	Shift-Command-S
Enter full-screen view	Control-Command-F
Hide or show sidebars on the right side of the Keynote window	Option-Command-I
Hide or show the toolbar	Option-Command-T
Hide Keynote	Command-H
Hide windows of other applications	Option-Command-H
Minimize a window	Command-M

Minimize all windows	Option-Command-M
Open a new document	Command-N
Open an existing document	Command-O
Open the Page Setup window	Shift-Command-P
Print a document	Command-P
Quit Keynote	Command-Q
Quit Keynote and keep windows open	Option-Command-Q
Rearrange an item in the toolbar	Command-drag
Redo the last action	Shift-Command-Z
Remove an item from the toolbar	Command-drag away from the toolbar
Return to actual size	Command-0
Save a document	Command-S
Save As	Option-Shift-Command-S
Show or hide layout boundaries	Shift-Command-L
Show or hide the ruler	Command-R
Show or hide the tab bar	Shift-Command-T
Show page thumbnails	Option-Command-P
Show the Colors window	Shift-Command-C
Start dictation	Press Fn twice
Undo the last action	Command-Z
Zoom in	Command-Right Angle Bracket (>)

Zoom out	Command-Left Angle Bracket (<)
Zoom to selection	Shift-Command-0

FORMATTING KEYBOARD SHORTCUTS

Action	Shortcut
Show the Fonts window	Command-T
Show the Colors window	Shift-Command-C
Apply boldface to selected text	Command-B
Apply italic to selected text	Command-I
Apply underline to selected text	Command-U
Make the font size bigger	Command-Plus Sign (+)
Make the font size smaller	Command-Minus Sign (-)
Make the text superscript	Control-Shift-Command-Plus Sign (+)
Make the text subscript	Control-Command-Minus Sign (-)
Insert an equation	Option-Command-E
Decrease the indent level of a list item	Shift-Tab
Increase the indent level of a list item	Tab
Turn text into a link	Command-K
Add a bookmark	Option-Command-B

Cut the selection	Command-X
Copy the selection	Command-C
Copy the paragraph style	Option-Command-C
Paste the selection	Command-V
Paste the paragraph style	Option-Command-V
Paste and match the style of the destination text	Option-Shift-Command-V
Copy the graphic style of text	Option-Command-C
Paste the graphic style of text	Option-Command-V
Add a range to (or remove it from) the selection	Shift-drag
Insert a nonbreaking space	Option-Space bar
Insert a line break (soft return)	Shift-Return
Insert a paragraph break	Return
Insert a new line after the insertion point	Control-O
Insert a page break	Fn-Command-Return
Enter special characters	Control-Command-Space bar
Transpose the characters on either side of the insertion point	Control-T
Add an EndNote bibliography	Shift-Option-Command-E

ABOUT THE AUTHOR

Scott La Counte is a librarian and writer. His first book, *Quiet, Please: Dispatches from a Public Librarian* (Da Capo 2008) was the editor's choice for the Chicago Tribune and a Discovery title for the Los Angeles Times; in 2011, he published the YA book The N00b Warriors, which became a #1 Amazon bestseller; his most recent book is *#OrganicJesus: Finding Your Way to an Unprocessed, GMO-Free Christianity* (Kregel 2016).

He has written dozens of best-selling how-to guides on tech products.

You can connect with him at ScottDouglas.org.

Printed in Great Britain
by Amazon